THE HOUSE THAT JACK BUILT

FREEWHEELING

HOMES

THE HOUSE THAT JACK BUILT

FREEWHEELING
HOMES

DAVID PEARSON

CHELSEA GREEN PUBLISHING COMPANY
WHITE RIVER JUNCTION, VERMONT

Series designer: Sara Mathews
Designer: Bridget Morley

First published in the United Kingdom in 2002 by
Gaia Books Ltd., 66 Charlotte Street, London W1T 4QE

Printed in Dubai. U.A.E.

First printing 2002

04 03 02 01   1 2 3 4 5

Library of Congress Cataloging-in-Publication Data available upon request.

Chelsea Green Publishing Company
Post Office Box 428
White River Junction, VT 05001
(800) 639-4099
www.chelseagreen.com

Cover image by Jay Shafer; page 2 by David Pearson; page 5 by Dan Wing

"To a life on the open road."

CONTENTS

H O M E S   O N   W H E E L S

"... THEY SAW A GYPSY CARAVAN, SHINING WITH NEWNESS, PAINTED A
CANARY-YELLOW PICKED OUT WITH GREEN, AND RED WHEELS.
'THERE YOU ARE!' CRIED THE TOAD, STRADDLING AND EXPANDING HIMSELF. 'THERE'S
REAL LIFE FOR YOU, EMBODIED IN A LITTLE CART. THE OPEN ROAD, THE DUSTY
HIGHWAY, THE HEATH, THE COMMON, THE HEDGEROWS, THE ROLLING DOWNS!
... HERE TODAY, UP AND OFF TO SOMEWHERE ELSE TOMORROW!'
... IT WAS INDEED VERY COMPACT AND COMFORTABLE. LITTLE SLEEPING BUNKS –
A LITTLE TABLE THAT FOLDED UP AGAINST THE WALL – A COOKING STOVE, LOCKERS,
BOOKSHELVES, A BIRD CAGE WITH A BIRD IN IT; AND POTS, PANS, JUGS AND KETTLES
OF EVERY SIZE AND VARIETY. 'ALL COMPLETE!' SAID THE TOAD TRIUMPHANTLY ..."

from *The Wind in the Willows* by Kenneth Grahame

"The essence of our wagon is its combination of sweetness and wild improbability, fantasy and utility, restfulness and motion." This is how modern wagon-builder Dan Wing (see page 76) sums up that special feeling that homes on wheels evoke. The open road is an archetypal image of freedom and adventure. Instead of the settled life, why not escape and find the excitement of new scenery and fresh faces? And why not travel in your own home with everything you need conveniently around you? Yes, life on the open road is the way to live, and how better than in the style and comfort of your own compact freewheeling home! Wherever you go and however foreign or strange the surroundings may be, you will always feel at home in your home on wheels.

But what can be the romance of the open road for the vacationer, was a very different story for the full-time travellers, such as Romany Gypsies. Until recently, travel was not an easy or pleasant experience. Before good roads existed few people ventured far afield. Some never even left the village where they were born! Nomadic peoples, who travelled to follow animal migrations or find new pasture for their flocks, had to transport goods and shelters on their backs or on dogs and pack animals. Wheels were no help in most terrain. Some people, however, did experiment in living in homes on wheels. The Scythians of the seventh century BC are said to have lived in wagons and, 800 years ago, Genghis Khan and his entourage travelled in large felt-covered yurts or *gers* mounted on ox-drawn carts.

Once a network of surfaced roads emerged in the early 1800s it became possible to travel with wheeled vehicles year round. This, plus bigger and stronger horses, opened up the way for both showfolk and Gypsies to travel widely in homes on wheels. Soon showfolk were living in specially built multi-use caravans that doubled as goods wagons and travelling theatres with raised stage and scenery. In *The Old Curiosity Shop*, written in 1840, Charles Dickens described how Mrs Jarley, the proprietress of a travelling waxworks show, had a living van with bed "after the fashion of a berth on board ship" complete with kitchen and stove. In time, showfolk commissioned special living vans such as the Burton (see page 53) from famous UK wagon-makers such as Orton and Spooner. Soon horse-drawn versions were superseded by longer, heavier metal-bodied vans – once such familiar features of the fairground and circus – towed by steam traction engines or trucks such as the Brayshaw (see page 33).

Gypsies were a distinct group of travellers. Descended from the Romany Gypsies of Central

THE PLEASURES OF LIFE CLOSE TO NATURE

Europe, they had a long history of nomadic life that revolved around rearing and trading horses. The word "Gypsies" comes from "Egyptians", as they were believed to have originated in Egypt, but study of the Romany language has found similarities with Indian dialects. Around 1000 years ago these people left India and journeyed slowly across to Europe, arriving in Britain in the 16th century.

The nomadic Gypsy lifestyle has always been regarded by the *Gaujo* (non-Gypsy) with a mixture of fascination and distrust. Wherever Gypsies went, they invariably suffered from harassment. In England, the Vagrancy Act of 1824 deemed anyone travelling in a cart or wagon who did not have

IN 1866 THE WANDERER, THE FIRST LEISURE VAN, IS MANHANDLED OFF SOFT GROUND.
FROM *CRUISE OF THE LAND YACHT "WANDERER"*, BY WILLIAM GORDON STABLES, 1886

a visible means of support to be a rogue or vagabond. Traditionally Gypsies earned money from horse dealing, peg and flower selling, fortune telling, household metalwork, and seasonal farm work. With the exception of horse dealing, most of these trades have disappeared, to be replaced with scrap dealing, tree lopping, and tarmacking.

Traditionally, until about the mid-19th century, Gypsies lived and cooked in "benders" (domed or tunnel-shaped temporary shelters made of bent rods or saplings, covered with canvas). But as roads improved and affordable wagons became available, some began to live in wagons they called *vardos*. The Bowtop (see page 35), with its canvas-covered hooped roof, is perhaps the best-known type. It is simple to build, light to pull, thrifty in materials, comfortable, and warm. The compact interior is entered by a half door at the front which allows the upper windows to be opened separately from the door beneath. A bunk bed built across the rear end, with a small window above, has a cupboard underneath for storing bedding in the day and for an extra sleeping space at night. Cupboards and shelves fill the side walls and the *vardo* is heated by a woodburning stove.

There were other types of *vardo*, from the lightweight Open-lot (see page 82) to the heavier Ledge (see page 61) or Cottage with its upright ribbed and boarded sides built on ledges over the wheels. Expensive *vardos* boasted fine carving both inside and out, painted, and often gilded with gold leaf. No wonder her *vardo* was a Gypsy woman's pride and joy!

The classic books by George Borrow, such as *Lavengro* published in 1851, spread the romance of the Gypsy way of life, but it was the Gypsy Lore Society, founded in 1888 (and now flourishing in the USA) that first fostered serious ethnological study. Today, everyone can taste this way of life by taking a leisurely vacation in a horse-drawn *vardo* (see Resources) or visiting annual horse fairs such as the Appleby Fair in Cumbria, England. Wagon enthusiasts such as Walter Lloyd, Gordon Boswell, and Andy Ball in the UK, and Dan Wing and Jim Tolpin in the USA, are keeping the Gypsy *vardo* alive in both traditional and modern forms.

ROLLING, ROLLING, ROLLING

When they crossed the country from East to West, 19th-century North American pioneers undertook one of the longest and most arduous journeys in American history. In what is often called the Great Migration, thousands of pioneers travelled from the bluffs of the Missouri River across the Great Plains, either to Santa Fe, or further over the Rockies and Sierras to California, and "Oregon Territory". From 1825 onward they journeyed in large horse- or mule-drawn covered wagons, called "prairie schooners", in long wagon trains. In a semi-military style, a party of 100 wagons would be divided into four sections, overseen by a lieutenant and with a captain in overall charge, plus guides and scouts. In addition to the sweltering heat and the lack of water, they braved many other obstacles, such as sand storms, river quicksands, prairie fires, hostile Indians, and stampeding buffalo. But once across the plains, new trials awaited them in the mountains beyond. Steep and treacherous trails, often blocked with rockfalls and mudslides, impeded progress. Controlling loaded wagons and horses in these conditions was extremely difficult. But worst of all was the weather and the prospect of being trapped in the mountains in deep snow during winter. This was the fate of the legendary Donner

Party who, in the winter of 1846–7, became stranded on the Truckee Route in the Sierra Nevada mountains, where they suffered dreadful privations. Totally unprepared for such harsh conditions, they gradually ran out of food and most of the party perished.

Today you can experience the excitement of the pioneer spirit in organized safety by signing up for specialist tours such as Hidden Trails (see page 72) for the covered wagon trip of your life.

LEISURE AND VINTAGE CARAVANS

The advent of motorized transport in the early 19th century encouraged the general public to travel much more widely than ever before. In about 1880, a Scottish eccentric, William Gordon Stables invented leisure caravanning in Britain. Known as the "gentleman Gypsy", he toured in great style in his elegant horse-drawn Wanderer caravan and wrote a book about his travels in his "land yacht" (see illustration on page 10). The Wanderer is still preserved in Bristol Museum, England. The idea soon became fashionable among the affluent and, as early as 1907, a group of enthusiasts formed the Caravan Club of Great Britain. Soon motor-drawn caravans overtook horse-drawn versions and many individuals and companies experimented with innovative practical and impractical models. During the 1920s (partly using knowledge and military construction techniques gained from WWI) caravans became lighter. Many also lost their upright box-on-wheels look and took on a more streamlined aerodynamic styling, echoing Art Deco fashion of the time. Famous UK models such as the Winchester (see page 70), the Raven, and the Cheltenham are legendary, but it was the Eccles firm who eventually came to dominate the industry and export all over the world.

In the USA, longer-distance travel, powerful automobiles, and the extremes of climate led to larger trailers with more onboard facilities, better insulation, and comfort control. As well as the classic Airstream trailers (see pages 38 and 68), other superb designs appeared such as the Shasta, Trotwood, Vagabond, and Spartan. From the 1930s onward, leisure caravanning grew in popularity and designs diversified, creating luxury caravans for one end of the market as well as lighter, smaller, and cheaper models (see page 26). These ultra-lights were often foldable or pop-up and designed in the aerodynamic "teardrop" style for easier towing by the smallest vehicle or even motorbike and sidecar combination.

Today, caravanning is one of the most popular leisure pursuits, and alongside the mainstream

Robert Croft

Gad-About
$135

*America's
Lowest Priced
House Trailer*

THE Gad-About House Trailer for 2 was developed and manufactured by Sears Roebuck and Company. When Sears decided to discontinue

THE GAD-ABOUT (ABOVE) AND THE RUNLITE DATING FROM 1927 (BELOW AND RIGHT) WERE BOTH DESIGNED IN THE POPULAR TEARDROP AERODYNAMIC SHAPE

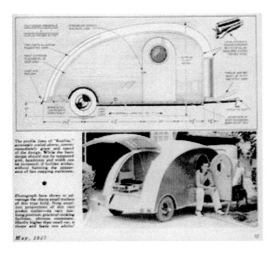

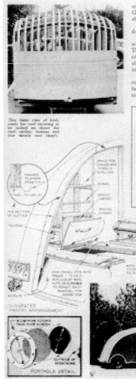

The Shoreland Tandem Town and Country, made by the Streamlite Corporation, was a great attraction at the 1947-48 Sport and Travel Show in Chicago, Illinois. Many of its innovative features later became industry standards, according to Donald Ham, who designed the 30-footer to match Chrysler's 1947 Town and Country convertible. Pretty stylish combination!

THE SHORELINE TANDEM 1947 – LUXURIOUS MODERN CARAVANNING IN POST-WAR AMERICA

world of modern travel trailers and motor homes, a growing number of enthusiasts are dedicated to saving and renovating the heritage of vintage caravans (see Resources).

THE SILVER PALACE

Who can forget the first Airstream trailer they ever saw? With its sleek and shiny streamlined body it evokes the very spirit of swift and easy travel across the vast spaces of the USA. You just want to hitch it up and go! Its creator, Wally Byam, is said to have coined the name Airstream because he felt his trailers cruised down the road "like a stream of air".

In 1935 Byam teamed up with William Hawley Bowlus, a pioneer airplane designer who was an expert in the stressed aluminium construction and streamlining of the airplane industry. The Bowlus Road Chief caravan had the bullet nose now characteristically associated with the Airstream, but had a rear door rather than the side door preferred in later Airstream models. The revolutionary Clipper was launched in 1936, with its monocoque aluminium body, internal water supply, enclosed galley, electric light, advanced insulation, and optional air conditioning system – a truly modern and aerodynamic caravan. Under Byam's direction the classic Airstream style evolved over the next 20 years to become the Cadillac of travel trailers, and by the 1950s models ranged from the compact Cruisette to the spacious Flying Cloud.

The classic bodystyle was continued until the launch of the new 1969 model, which then lasted well into the 1990s. During this period even larger and more luxurious models emerged, such as the Ambassador and the Excella. Although Wally Byam died in 1962, his innovation, inspiration, and heritage lives on. The company continued to bring out new models, such as the ever-popular Land Yacht motorhome. Today, the Wally Byam Caravan Club International and the Vintage Airstream Club foster large networks of "Airstreamers", who are the proud owners of both vintage and modern Airstreams in North America and around the world. When Wally Byam began to build trailers in his backyard in the 1930s, little did he think that he was creating one of America's living legends – the Airstream!

THE ELECTRIC KOOL-AID ACID TEST
It was in the spirit of Jack Kerouac's *On The Road* that Ken Kesey and his "Merry Pranksters" drove from New York to San Francisco in 1964 in a dayglo schoolbus. It not only celebrated the "hippy revolution" but gave a whole new meaning to freewheeling homes. Suddenly, hastily adapted and brightly painted vehicles of every description – buses, trucks, and ambulances – were everywhere on the highways going West. Surely the psychedelic VW camper van (with surfboard on roof) is the Californian icon of that time? A new generation was living and roving around in homes on wheels.

Since the 1960s what was "counter culture" has shifted to "tribal culture" and, for some, this has meant a more nomadic lifestyle. With little chance of jobs or housing, they feel themselves to be economic refugees fleeing from society to find a new way. For many travellers this means taking to the road to travel with family and others in any vehicle that can make a home (see pages 24 and 56). Often suffering much the same persecution as Gypsies did in an earlier era, they stay on roadside sites until they are moved on, or find respite for a while at a New Age festival, fair, or gathering.

For basic guidance on finding, renovating, or building your home on wheels, see the Make It section (page 80) and the Resources section (page 92) for useful companies and contacts. Whether you choose a vintage caravan, Gypsy *vardo*, converted bus, or Airstream trailer, start now to find your freewheeling home!

SMALL IS BEAUTIFUL

Jay Shafer: In the US, constructing small houses is not only uncommon, it's illegal. For the past few decades, anyone wanting to build a small home in a populated area has probably run up against minimum size standards. This was my main reason for incorporating wheels into my home's design. Minimum size standards govern the size of houses — not travel trailers — and so, by putting my house (known as Tumbleweed) on wheels, I was able to circumvent these antiquated laws.

The intention of these minimum size standards is to preserve the property values of larger houses by keeping unsightly little hovels from popping up in the neighborhood. But the result of these well-intentioned codes has been inordinate consumption of natural resources and increased production of construction waste and emissions through building larger houses, a lack of affordable housing and, of course, large unsightly hovels.

It has been said that the best way to subvert a system of imposed excess is by living simply. With this in mind, I built my house to show that bigger isn't necessarily better. At 130 square feet (12 sq m), Tumbleweed has consumed far fewer resources and produced far less pollution than an American house of a more standard size. In addition, Tumbleweed cost only about one-fifth as much as the average home. With $42,000 I was able to put five times as much money per square foot into quality materials and construction than is generally allowed for a typical house. I could have built it for much less, but I succumbed to the urge to invest some

JAY SHAFER

BUILT IN A WIND-RESISTANT CAPE COD STYLE, TUMBLEWEED ALLOWS A SIMPLE UNPOLLUTING LIFESTYLE.
IN THIS SMALL HOME EVERY CUBIC INCH IS USED TO ITS FULL POTENTIAL

JAY SHAFER

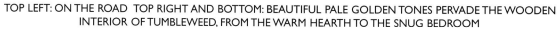

TOP LEFT: ON THE ROAD TOP RIGHT AND BOTTOM: BEAUTIFUL PALE GOLDEN TONES PERVADE THE WOODEN
INTERIOR OF TUMBLEWEED, FROM THE WARM HEARTH TO THE SNUG BEDROOM

of the money saved on quantity into quality. I do not regret it. I consider that one of the greatest joys of a small house is the opportunity to develop its every cubic inch meticulously in a way that is generally not possible with a larger space.

Still, my main reason for building such a small home was neither financial nor environmental. Mostly, I just like the convenience of a small home. Extra space requires extra time for cleaning and upkeep that, quite honestly, I would rather spend on other endeavors. I simply do not want to spend the rest of my life paying for and maintaining more than I need to be happy.

The form of Tumbleweed is no more complicated than the lifestyle it allows me. The gravity-fed shower and kitchen sink, the composting toilet and photovoltaic electric system (including lights, fans, a stereo, and a television and video recorder) meet my needs without exceeding them. The house's overall structure is nothing fancy. It's really just an amalgamation of some of the most common architectural forms of this country. Its unadorned exterior (designed to combat wind resistance on the road) was inspired by the Cape Cod style (designed to withstand ocean gales). Tumbleweed's proportions and symmetries are direct descendants of the formal tradition. The foundation comes straight from what has been called America's most modern vernacular form — the mobile home. It is, in short, not the product of invention but of evolution — its every part empirically proven to work well and withstand the test of time.

RECLAIMING MY HERITAGE

Gordon Boswell: I come from a long line of the Romany family name of Boswell, one of the oldest Romany names. I can trace my family back to the early 1700s.

I was born in 1940, and in my early years we travelled the country in Gypsy wagons and horses. It was around that time and a little later that some of the first Romany people got out of the Gypsy wagons, and moved into the new trailer caravans of that period. We all moved on, but as a young man my days in the horse-drawn wagon were always in my mind, and I never forgot them.

As time went by, more and more Romany families went into the modern trailer caravan, and I personally felt sorry for the old wagons being left to rot in the fields and back of hedges.

Even some *Gaujo* people, not Gypsy people, would buy one from the Romanies to use in their gardens for the children to play in, and to be used as an extra room. Whenever I saw one I would find out who it belonged to and try and buy it. I worked hard to bring the wagons back to life again by restoring and painting them.

My collection grew. Some people even said, "Take it away, it will only be used for firewood." As we restored one or two of them, we took them out on the road again. My wife Margaret and I, and the children, started to use them to go up to Appleby Horse Fair in Cumbria. We first did this journey from Spalding to Appleby 23 years ago – a distance of 280 miles (450 km). We travelled in my father's footsteps, as he had done this journey years before.

BARRIE LAW

GORDON AND MARGARET BOSWELL PREPARE A ROMANY MEAL, ON THE ROAD IN A RESTORED *VARDO*

By travelling in these wagons, we got known through newspaper reports and television, and people asked me to go out and give talks on the journey to Appleby, which I did and still do. I would give them a talk on the history of the Romany people, and I would show slides of the journey. They would then ask me questions after, which I would be pleased to answer.

I was giving more and more talks, and an idea came into my mind to open a Romany Museum, in Spalding, Lincolnshire, so the public could come and see my collection of Romany *vardos* and memorabilia. I opened the Museum in the memory of my father Syveste Gordon Boswell on the 25 February 1995, which would have been his 100th birthday. He died in 1977, aged 82 years. The museum has grown and we cater mainly for coach parties – our theatre room seats more than 60. The visit lasts two hours and they have a slide show of one of our journeys from Spalding to Appleby, followed by tea and biscuits.

I talk of how the Romanies lived in *vardos*. A large family would have two wagons and a tent. The tent had two uses: by day, a kitchen and living area; by night, an extra bedroom. All cooking was done outside on the open fire. The food they ate was killed by their lurcher dogs – hares, rabbits, pheasants, partridges, and of course hedgehog – then cooked in stews in the big boiler, fried in the large frying pan, or spit-roasted over the fire.

We also take people on the road to experience life in the *vardo*, but we cook them steak instead of hedgehog!

BARRIE LAW

GORDON BOSWELL

TOP: GORDON AND MARGARET ON A JOURNEY TO APPLEBY
BOTTOM: THE LOVINGLY RESTORED *VARDOS* AT GORDON'S ROMANY MUSEUM, SPALDING, ENGLAND

A REWARDING WAY OF LIFE

Amalia: We have lived on the road for about 10 years. We built a bowtop on to a trailer base and that's what we live in. It's got little windows and stable doors, and is very comfortable inside. There's a big double bed raised up at one end, and underneath that is Emerald's bedroom.

John is a blacksmith, a journeyman, really. He did a smithying course at college and an apprenticeship after that. Now we travel about and he takes work as he finds it. His main work is with the timber framers where he makes the pins that hold the big house beams together. He also does agricultural work – picking mainly – in the itinerant farmworker tradition. We're allowed to park up in the farmer's yard or down a lane somewhere and then, when the season for work comes around, the pickers are close at hand. If we stick around at night we act as night watchmen as well.

I do a bit of crafts and selling, and support the home. Emerald is home-schooled, but our life on the road is an education in itself.

It's a really rewarding lifestyle. You don't get bored of the view as you're always moving on. We have to collect our firewood and water. The vehicle has a woodburning stove, which keeps it nice and toasty. The truck is very economical to heat as it's a very small space. We have solar panels on the roof which run lights and a stereo. Generally, houses use up more resources to build. Heat, light, and water usage is much higher than our family use. Environmentally, this is a sounder way of life.

INGRID CRAWFORD

TOP: JOHN, AMALIA, AND EMERALD'S TRUCK HITCHED TO THE BOWTOP BOTTOM LEFT: EMERALD AND FRIEND
IN THE BOWTOP BOTTOM RIGHT: THE KITCHEN AREA INSIDE THE BOWTOP

THE BERKELEY CARAVETTE

Steve Pepper: I used to own a Berkeley T60 car, which was very small and cramped with all our camping gear for our weekend rally trips. It pulled a rare lightweight Raleigh folding caravan, but the only information I could find on the Raleigh was a photocopy of an original advert from the early 1960s. As each rally brought new admirers, I became aware that a wide range of very small caravans and campers had been produced since the 1930s. We collectively described these craft as "microcaravans", and have used the name ever since.

Friends said that I was becoming obsessed, and it wouldn't surprise them if I started a magazine. For a laugh, *Microcaravan News* was born, with a small circulation of readers in several countries. People were soon sending me old cuttings and reports, and ringing to tell me of vans for sale and wanted. This information is archived into the International Register of Microcaravans (IROM).

We continued to use the Raleigh regularly but it was becoming a pain to put up. So when I heard about a Berkeley Caravette for sale, I checked the archive for the specifications, which, with a test drive, convinced me this would be more practical. I stripped the Caravette and sprayed it red to match my 2CV. It's small, but it doesn't need to be put up and down all the time.

Through an internet search on microcaravans we discovered that the Americans had a 60-year history of producing "Teardrop Trailers". These probably influenced Charles Panter's basic Caravette design.

STEVE SPRAYED HIS SMALL AND COMPACT BERKELEY CARAVETTE RED TO MATCH
THE RED CAR HE USES TO TOW IT

THE ROLLS ROYCE OF LIVING VANS

Anna Carter: Contemporary living always seems to have eluded me. I've moved from living in a chilly, gas-lit Victorian house with inadequate plumbing, to a Medieval Hall with no plumbing, to my present home, a 30-foot (9 m) showman's van.

The van was built by the Vosper shipyard in 1948. I think there was a lull in ship production at this time. When we restored the van in 1985 we took off the panels and revealed woodwork with *Fore & Aft* pencilled on it.

The van is late Art Deco, with the wild extravagance of a huge marble fireplace, which causes the van to lean slightly on one side. The interior is wood with cut-glass windows. There are never any decisions to make about wallpaper when you live in a van, you just need a big tin of polish.

This radical change in lifestyle came about through my late husband's collecting habit. In 1976, John saw and fell in love with a neglected fairground ride – a set of galloping horses. I'd seen that glazed look in his eyes before, but this was the most ambitious project so far. It drained all our energy and financial resources and was the foundation stone of the "Carter Royal Berkshire Steam Fair" that now travels around London and the Home Counties. We have the biggest collection of vintage rides and attractions, and also the largest number of old showman's vans.

We live in these vans all year, although we are only on tour for seven months from Easter to October. Living in a van makes you much more aware of the passing seasons. You hear the rain pounding on the roof and feel the

BRIAN STEPTOE

**ANNA'S 1948 VOSPER LIVING VAN IS TOWED BY A VINTAGE SCAMMELL LORRY
ON HERSHAM VILLAGE GREEN, MIDDLESEX, ENGLAND**

first signs of autumn. In the winter the vans are a haven of warmth, with a coal stove burning.

In the early days our five children slept on bunks, pull-out settees, and shortened cots in our 22-foot (7 m) van. We had gas lighting, and this is where my expertise came in. I knew all about the intricate workings of gas mantles! We cooked meals on a gas stove and washed up in a bowl. All the water had to be collected from the nearest tap in stainless steel water cans.

The children's childhood was unconventional – no time was spent watching breakfast TV. When we bought the longer van the extra space supplied a kitchen – the height of luxury. Still no modern conveniences, but room to sit around a tiny table.

BRIAN STEPTOE

Now all the children have left home except my teenage daughter Rosie. She has never lived in a house and never wants to. She claims they make strange noises, and is happy to accept her tiny living space. She can walk out of the door and visit her brothers, nieces, and nephews and all her friends. This is the advantage of our lifestyle. If you tire of one neighbour, you can have another next week!

My sons all have their own vans that they share with their families. The girls miss hot baths and flush toilets and washing machines, but the children all play together every day, which has its own compensations, and we all have a new town to visit each week for some retail therapy.

Apart from the van we live in I own a 1927 Brayshaw. This is a Rolls Royce

BRIAN STEPTOE

ABOVE: THE SITTING ROOM WITH FITTED STOVE AND CUT-GLASS MIRROR, LOOKING TOWARD THE BEDROOM
FACING PAGE: THE RESTORED CEILING WITH ITS ORIGINAL DESIGN OF ROSES, BIRDS, AND GOLD SCROLLWORK

of a van, the interior is breathtaking, with painted ceilings of sky, roses, birds, and butterflies. The ceiling was obscured by blackened varnish, but I started to clean it with meths one day, revealing these amazing paintings. It became an obsession, I spent weeks in there getting high on meths and probably killing millions of brain cells. The result was well worth it; this van is my special, grandchild-free zone.

The advantages of van dwelling are the adventure of moving, the close proximity of chosen family and friends, the spontaneous barbeques and social events. Also, living with the job is essential. The disadvantages are lack of space, the effort of packing all your belongings down once a week, and the lack of access to modern conveniences. No-one who lives as we do ever takes water for granted, it's always used carefully. I'm horrified by house dwellers who waste so much of this precious commodity.

We are considered rather quaint by the rest of the travelling fraternity. Showfolk now have "state of the art" vans – huge, with "pull outs" to increase the size, and with every modern convenience installed. Vans like these are tempting but would not complement our Vintage Fair.

Looking back over 25 years, we've had many adventures travelling the long distances from show to show. It has sometimes been a hard life, but never boring.

I suppose I'll have to give it all up one day when I can't climb up the wagon steps to my front door.

Hopefully, not quite yet.

BRIAN STEPTOE

ANNA CARTER WITH HER RESTORED 1927 BRAYSHAW LIVING VAN

THE HORSE COMES FIRST

Walter Lloyd: When I grew up there were working horses on farms and pulling delivery vehicles in the country – the greengrocer, butcher, and fishmonger all came round with a horse and cart. My family and I also travelled from time to time with a donkey and cart, or with pack donkeys. I started breeding Fell Ponies in the late 1950s and used them for farm work. I first owned a Bowtop Wagon in 1960, and started to help build them in 1978. I built the first on my own in 1986, and since then I have lived in wagons all the year round.

A Bowtop is a horse-drawn Gypsy caravan with four wheels and a canvas covered roof, fastened to the wooden bows that give it its name. This design is very light, making it easy for a horse to pull, as you will discover when you come to your first hill! Generally, a horse or pony can pull its own weight up a hill of 1 in 8. Any steeper, and it will need help from a second horse, a "sideliner". So, the weight of the wagon is important, not only the "dray" it is built on, and the woodwork of the "top", but also the food, cooking gear, clothes, harness, and everything else.

You learn to take a minimum of things with you – spare breeching straps for the harness become more important than that pair of tidy shoes. Waterproofs are worth having – huddling wet and shivering by a camp fire of wet wood that won't burn is not much fun. When you choose a place to stop, it has to have grass and water for the horses before anything else, then shelter and firewood. Shops and pubs come after the welfare of the horses.

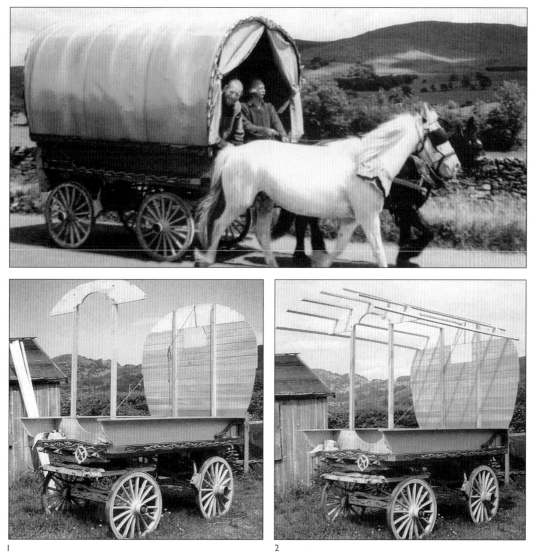

WALTER LLOYD

1   2

TOP: PONIES HADES HILL OSCAR (BLACK GELDING) WITH BETH (GREY MARE) SIDELINING
BOTTOM: (1) THE FRONT AND REAR CROWN BOARDS ARE FITTED (2) AND THEN THE RUNNERS

WALTER LLOYD

(3) THE SIDE PLANKS AND FRONT FORMERS (4) THE SOAKED BOWS ARE CURVED AND SCREWED INTO PLACE
(5) CHECKED LINING COVERS THE BOWS (6) AN INSULATION LAYER IS COVERED WITH GREEN CANVAS

It really helps to drive a light pony and cart before you buy or build a wagon, to get some driving experience. There are not very many really old Bowtops about. Most that you will see have been built in the last 20 years or so by people in their backyards, but some are still built by professional wagon-builders and wheelwrights.

If you are building or buying, the first thing to consider is the dray, or four-wheeled cart, that it is built on. A typical full-size dray will have a floor 9 feet long by 5 feet wide (2.7 by 1.5 m), with rear wooden wheels of 33 inches (85 cm) diameter, making the floor about 4 feet (120 cm) above the ground. A small one might be 6 inches (15 cm) shorter and narrower, with 31 inch (79 cm) wheels. This small difference makes it a lot lighter. I use Parana pine and cedar for most of the woodwork, because it's light and strong so I can use planking only half an inch (1.2 cm) thick.

The place to see Bowtops is at Horse Fairs, especially in the north of England. I travel to Appleby Horse Fair every year, and usually see 80 to a 100 Bowtops on the road, many newly built. You can see the wagons travelling to and from the Fair from late May to the middle of June, especially on the road from Kirkby Lonsdale through Kirkby Stephen, and south on the A66 road from County Durham and Northumberland. Catch their drivers in a pub in the evenings, and you can't stop them talking! Try "The Head" at Middleton, south of Sedbergh, or the "Fat Lamb" at Ravenstonedale.

See you up the road!

THE WALLY BYAM WAY OF LIFE

Esther Garrison: As a child I used to dream of far-away places. Little did I know that I would have the chance to travel around the world, and visit fifty-six foreign countries. Most of this came about through owning an Airstream travel trailer and belonging to the Wally Byam Caravan Club International.

Clay and I bought our first Airstream in 1957. Our first rally was attending the Mid West Unit at Champaign, Illinois. At that time there were 37 members in the nine-state region and 35 of us were at that rally.

In 1958 we were in Mexico City to hear Wally Byam's plans for a caravan tour of Central America. Wally said to the meeting: "If you have adventure in your heart, go. If not, stay home."

We had the pleasure and honor of traveling with Wally Byam as far as the roads would take us in Central America at that time. The trip was shown on Bold Adventure TV. We put our Airstreams on a flat car train ride for 175 miles (280 km), we towed them over 295 miles (475 km) mostly on rock and gravel roads, through 36 rivers and over 11,000 ft (350 m) mountains, from San Jose in Costa Rica to Managua in Nicaragua.

Where there were no road signs we threw out bags of flour to signal which direction to go. In one of these areas we took a wrong turn and went through a river, but couldn't make it due to sand and the steep incline. Our car plus a big four-wheel-drive truck couldn't tow it out, so after many hours of trying Clay tied a rope to the front of the car and about 100 Guatemalans pulled us out. We got into camp that

ESTHER GARRISON

TOP: WALLY BYAM CARAVAN TO CANADA, NEAR QUEBEC CITY – AN ANNUAL EVENT SINCE 1954
BOTTOM LEFT: NO ROAD! BOTTOM RIGHT: RIVER CROSSING, 1958 CARAVAN TO CENTRAL AMERICA

evening at about 11pm, glad to see some of the group waiting with a pot of tea. Several didn't make it into camp that night, including Wally Byam!

Some of the highlights of our travels were having tea with the President of Costa Rica in his palace, and attending an International Ball put on by the President of Honduras.

We have traveled in Australia for two months by car and trailer, with our good friends Erma and Barney Wilkins. In the outback country the heat was stifling — the temperatures reached 107°F (42°C). We encountered over-whelming humidity, hundreds of dead cattle, and even a fellow Ohian. One day we counted over 150 kangaroos. The worst was the millions of flies. You couldn't even eat a sandwich without putting on a fly net.

We toured France on Caravan America using cars and trailers from the French Automobile Club. And we have traveled in the UK a number of times, with Edna and Laurie Simmons as English leaders. On one occasion in Scotland six out of our nine rented trailers blew over in a terrible storm. Five of them had to be replaced, but luckily no-one was hurt.

I could go on about our trips, but really the most important point about our travels is the Airstream Club. It's been the greatest thing that could have happened to us. If Wally were here today, we would thank him personally for helping to make our travel dreams come true.

God has been good to us. He has granted us Health, Happiness, and the Wally Byam Way of Life.

ESTHER GARRISON

CARAVAN WITH WALLY BYAM TO MEXICO IN 1958 – FOR THOSE WITH ADVENTURE IN THEIR HEARTS

SOMETHING BETWEEN A RAILWAY CARRIAGE
AND A TRAVELLER'S VAN

John Shervell: In the early 1960s when I was a young boy, farm labour was cheap and plentiful, and villages were always bustling with all kinds of activities. The men working on my father's 560-acre (225 ha) farm were busily employed at ploughing, drilling, milking, handling grain, or looking after sheep. There was always plenty to do, and plenty of men to do it.

The shepherd was a very insular man who found it hard to mix with the other staff on the farm. He would spend many days and weeks on his own just tending the flocks of sheep. All his work would be done out in the fields, except at shearing time, when the whole flock would be taken up to an isolated barn, which had a sheep dip and carrels to guide the stock into the correct places.

During lambing in the early spring, the shepherd had a shed on wheels which resembled something between a railway carriage and a traveller's van. Its purpose was mainly for shelter, and for storing equipment and medicines. The shepherd's work was hard and often carried out in some atrocious weather, and the hut was there for him to eat, rest, and even sleep in during that time.

Methods of farming changed, and the shepherd's hut became redundant and was parked up in a corner of the yard and left there. As children we would use it as a camp and play and amuse ourselves there for hours.

Now, as farming gradually seems to be fading into oblivion, and it becomes a struggle to survive, we are told we must diversify into other projects. So I looked at what was left of the old hut

JOHN SHERVELL

and thought that if I wanted one, so might others. I measured it up to find out the sizes of timber used and how the steering worked, and got castings made of the wheels. All the metal work I did myself, as I once trained and worked as a blacksmith.

I now make the Shepherd's Huts to order. Each one is constructed as an exact copy of the original one. The chassis and entire framework is made from good quality grade softwood, treated with modern preservatives. The hut is fully insulated between the timber cladding on the inside and the plastisol coated corrugated tin, which is on the outside. The windows are double-glazed, and electricity cabling and telephone lines can be installed, thus bringing this traditional style hut into the 21st century.

TOP: SHEPHERD'S HUT IN THE FIELD, READY FOR A VISITOR
BELOW: BUNK BEDS IN THE TIMBER-CLAD INTERIOR

EURO VOYAGING

Carol: In March 1991 my partner John, who was a self-employed joiner, was finding his workload dwindling. One day he said "If I haven't got any work I might as well be 'not working' abroad." We decided we would set out for Europe with Ashley (9), Melanie (7), and Tom, our four-month-old baby.

The next day, John went trawling around the local bus companies in search of our new home. It didn't take long to find a redundant bus for sale at £1500. Named "Euro Voyager", this bus had to be the one for us.

John had converted and lived in a bus before, and knew how it had to be done. There was one basic rule: nothing should convert into anything else. You shouldn't have to wash up before you can brush your teeth, or clear the table before you turn it into your bed.

John organized barn space from a local farmer, and set to work stripping and converting the bus.

He started with the living space, keeping two pairs of seats — one from each side of the bus — and putting them face to face. He then built a table in between. On the opposite "wall" from the dining table John built the galley area with full-size sink and drainer, kitchen cupboards, and a full-size gas cooker. He also found and installed a second-hand caravan fridge that would run on batteries or gas.

John's skill with wood made the project much easier. Walls were built out of tongue-and-groove panelling. In the children's bedroom, Ashley and Melanie had bunk beds and Tom's cot was screwed to the floor. At the back of the bus was the master bedroom.

THE GALLEY AREA WITH ALL MODERN CONVENIENCES – INCLUDING A FULL-SIZE GAS COOKER

JOHN RATCLIFFE

Two domestic-sized water tanks were installed in the boot. When a tap was turned on, the pump kicked in automatically. Our power was supplied by industrial-strength batteries stored in the side lockers on the outside of the bus. The shower was full size, although we had to have a chemical toilet and a tiny caravan-style basin. Water was heated by a two-gallon (9-litre) gas heater – enough for a good shower at the very least.

Ten weeks after the idea was born, we set sail from Portsmouth, England, for Cherbourg, France. That summer we enjoyed cheap wine and good food in France. In Spain, we saw thousands of olive trees as we crossed the Pyrenees and hugged the coast as far as Valencia, before heading across country towards Portugal. We made many friends en route and John even found some work.

Our long summer came to an end and we made our way back through Spain, France, and Switzerland to Germany. We bought a beautiful woodburning stove in France, as we could foresee cold nights ahead. Sure enough, in the Black Forest in Germany we found ourselves in the mountains, in snow. In November we returned through The Netherlands and took the ferry back to Harwich, England.

Coming home after such a long adventure was not easy. After a few months we sold our bus to a young couple who planned to take it to India with their baby. As I followed our home on wheels when we delivered it to them, I found myself in floods of tears. It had been such a big part of our lives.

JOHN RATCLIFFE

TOP LEFT: THE EURO VOYAGER TOP RIGHT: THE WOODBURNING STOVE KEEPS THE BUS WARM AND COSY
BOTTOM LEFT: THE KITCHEN-DINER BOTTOM RIGHT: BROTHERS ENJOYING A BEDTIME STORY

BUILDING TRADITIONAL WAGONS

Andy Ball: I got into wagon-building in 1983 when I chose to copy a "Bill Wright" Bowtop design from around 1900 from *The English Gypsy Caravan* by C.H. Ward-Jackson and Denis E. Harvey. It took me six months to make, but unfortunately the scale drawings proved inaccurate, and my wagon came out slightly oversized.

Nevertheless, I set off to tour Dorset and Somerset for two summers with Punch, a chestnut Suffolk and Welsh cob cross, and Blue, a lurcher with shocking habits and a voracious appetite. Punch could pull the waggon away from standing with the brakes full on and large stones placed under each back wheel. I'd often have to run like the clappers to catch up with him and the terrified Blue. We had many traffic incidents, like the time

I found myself chasing Punch and my home down the wrong side of a busy road in Bridport. In the end, I had to resort to tying his knees together whenever we needed a short stop.

The importance of finding a pitch to stop for the night was always a priority. A good pitch meant plenty of space for Punch on his tether and a close supply of water. I was always reluctant to pass a good pitch by simply because it was too early in the day, so some days we only travelled 3 miles (5 km) to the next pitch and stayed for the night.

Motorways, surprisingly, provided a good source of pitches as they often cut right through some of the old, smaller roads. This created a lonely cul-de-sac to park in, with water from nearby cattle troughs in the fields, which was welcome, despite the noise.

ANDY IS STILL RENOVATING HIS HOME – THIS 1899 SHOWMAN'S RAIL VAN

ANDY BALL

Many adventures later, I wound up living in that Bowtop behind a small Cotswold brewery, and with some adjustments to the scale drawings I drifted into making wagons full-time. It has been known for a customer to turn up on the doorstep and offer to buy the wagon I was living in. I've sold two right out from under me.

I build five main styles of wagon: the Reading, Ledge, Burton, Bowtop, and Open-lot. The first three are wooden-sided and roofed, and the last two are basically canvas stretched over a latticework of steam-bent ash laths. The Bowtop and Open-lot are probably the most practical wagons for travel, due to their inherent stability and lightness. The wooden-sided wagons, with their acres of chamfered ribs and very elaborately

TOP: ETCHED GLASS IN THE WINDOWS, GOLD SCROLLING AND MAHOGANY
CABINETS IN THE INTERIOR   BOTTOM: A GOOD NIGHT'S SLEEP

ANDY BALL

THE LEDGE, WITH ITS DECORATIVE TOUCHES AND ELEGANT WHEELS, IS A TRULY STUNNING SIGHT

hand-carved porch brackets, make ready platforms for some really fancy decorative paintwork.

Probably the most satisfying wagon to make is the Ledge, so named because it is wider above the wheels, creating an overhang or "ledge". This increases the width considerably to 6 foot 6 inches (2 m), so the bed, which goes across the back, is long enough for a reasonable night's sleep.

The Ledge's shape, coupled with its spindle-turned bantam cages over the front wheels, decorative spindle-turned cratch (a sort of rear-mounted luggage rack), and 5-foot (1.5 m) diameter rear wheels, make it a truly stunning sight.

The undercarriage is mostly ash, with elm for wheel hubs and oak for spokes. The forecarriage can be as complicated as you like, with elaborate chamfers and unnecessary curves all over the place. When you get to floor level, you change to softwood for lightness and complete the rest in this material. Sides are made of "penny-boarding" – a narrow matchboard – nailed to chamfered ribs mortised into top and bottom rails.

The roof is matchboard covered with canvas and a raised and glazed centre section or "Mollycroft". The interior is then fitted out with fireplace, bed, lockers, and glazed cabinets, all usually grained in mahogany.

The exterior is painted by my son Daniel, an accomplished wagon-painter. The chamfers are picked out in contrasting colours, then lined in cream or gold. The chamfers are chiselled hollows, ostensibly decorating the ribs of the Ledge to reduce the overall

ANDY BALL

A BURTON WAGON PAINTED IN TRADITIONAL COLOURS, WITH THE CHAMFERS PICKED OUT
AND LINED TO CONTRAST WITH THE MAIN BODY

weight of the wagon. The traditional scrolls designed for the entire wagon are painted freehand to suit the spaces they riot over, almost too much for the eye to take in. We choose traditional colours for the wagons, either Crimson Lake (a dark red) or green, with gold, unless someone requests their own special colour.

In 1999, I bought a dilapidated 22-foot (6.7 m) railvan, built by Jones of Hereford in 1899. These wagons were horse-drawn to the local railway station, then proceeded by rail to their destination, usually a fair or circus. This wagon was in a sorry state, with little roof left and no interior. I moved in once I had completed the roof, and I've been renovating it ever since. Daniel has grained the interior for me in mahogany and we've learned how to etch glass, so all the windows are highly decorated. The van is heated by a magnificent Godin stove, in a tiled and wood-carved fireplace.

I've been fascinated by camera obscuras ever since visiting the Bristol Observatory as a child. Over the years I have experimented with installing them in the wagons, wasting a lot of money on lenses which didn't work. The first one, in a wagon we rented out, projected the image on to an opposite wall. The holiday children stood on their heads to see the inverted image of the road and traffic behind them, as the wagon trundled along. I've installed one in my van, so when the sun is shining I can watch exciting things, like chickens scratching and sleeping dogs, on a circular screen at one darkened end of the caravan.

ANDY BALL

DETAIL OF THE HAND-CARVED PORCH BRACKETS IN THE TRADITIONAL COLOURS

SPINNING ALONG

Sam: I travelled for seven years in horse-drawn vehicles, mostly in Somerset, Dorset, Devon, Hampshire, Wiltshire, and Wales. I first had a spinner: a two-wheeled cart.

When my daughter, Joya, was born I built a wagon, which made life easier. When we arrived, I could just throw a few things out and get the kettle on, instead of building a bender and unloading the cart each time we stopped. The floor was 8 feet by 5 feet (2.5 m by 1.5 m). It really bowed out, so that above our heads it was 7 feet (2 m) wide with about 5 inches (13 cm) of headroom. Loads of space and loads of light, with windows at the back.

I loved living close to nature and the changing seasons, watching and understanding the weather patterns. Collecting wood and water was also a very simple way of connecting to nature and the very basics of living. Wood was mostly plentiful and we're not short of water in Britain – springs were always a blessing. Joya loved living out. I collected material from the hedgerows and made baskets for a living. Selling them by the wagon and horses made an attractive scene.

It was sometimes tiring and lonely to travel alone or with just a few. It was better with the support of a community of people, who could all contribute to the quality of life. Winters could be hard, especially with the mud! It's a great environmental choice, but not many do it for long in Britain. There needs to be more land available and a bigger, committed community group doing it, in order to make a creative, fun, and self-sufficient semi-nomadic

INGRID CRAWFORD

SAM DRIVING HER SPINNER. A BENDER OR TENT IS PUT UP EACH NIGHT TO SERVE AS A BEDROOM

LIVING IN A WORK OF ART

Jim Tolpin: For more than 30 years I've made my living as a woodworker – mostly doing boatbuilding and custom cabinets. In the last ten years or so, I've also done technical writing about woodworking and architectural design. Over the course of these years, I've built five caravans – cozy living spaces on wheels. These vans, made of wood and canvas on a steel chassis, are not styled or constructed at all like typical recreational vehicle (RV) travel trailers, but more like the *vardos* of the Gypsies in the late 1800s in England (mostly), or the covered wagons of the Basque sheepherders of the American West.

In fact, I looked at many photos and examples of those wagons while I was developing my designs. I liked the simplicity of the sheepherder wagons, but I was also drawn to the woodworking and design challenges of the Gypsy wagons – so you can see the Gypsy influences in all my caravans. The big difference between my caravans and those of the Gypsies is that mine are designed to be towed behind a car or light truck. So my vans use standard trailer running gear, or truck chassis.

Construction and design are based largely on marine practices. Materials are chosen for corrosion and rot resistance. Exterior woods are mostly cedars, mahogany, and teak. This is just like traditional construction of a deck house on a sailing ship. All paints and caulking materials are marine grade. These are expensive choices, of course, but necessary for the caravans to endure life in the elements.

RV'ers aren't interested in these wagons without all the modern

JIM TOLPIN

JIM'S WAGON DESIGN IS INSPIRED BY GYPSY *VARDOS* AND BASQUE SHEEPHERDERS' COVERED WAGONS

conveniences. I don't put bathrooms in them, and there are only minimal cooking facilities. Plus, for the amount of space relative to a typical RV, my wagons are expensive – very expensive. But all that doesn't stop a certain type of person: the person who wants to live in a work of art. It is someone who wants to live not surrounded by plastic and aluminium, but instead with the rich textures, colors, and smells of real wood, leather, and fine fabrics. It's the person who wants a space for the three most important R's of life: reading, 'riting, and resting!

If they want to travel with the wagon, I suggest they get a van fitted out with kitchen and bathroom for the tow vehicle – that way all those messy/smelly activities can be taken care of outside the caravan. The Gypsies never used their caravans for those activities either.

For short periods of time I've lived in my own wood and canvas caravans and in typical metal and plastic travel trailers. I hated the latter and loved the former. In the RV, I felt insulated from the outside world – somehow the envelope of steel and plastic mutes my senses, deadens my sense of joy and wonder. In my caravans, I'm surrounded by materials that are living. The wood breathes and moves, creaking sometimes in the wind. Plant oils give the wood a rich, aromatic patina. The canvas roof lets in the light of both the sun and the moon. The wood stove exudes the rich smells of fruit wood burning, teas boiling, and herbs drying in the rack above. Here my mind expands and my heart feels at home.

JIM TOLPIN

TOP LEFT: INSIDE A LEDGE-STYLE VAN TOP RIGHT: THE ELEGANTLY DRAPED SLEEPING AREA
IN THE TINKER'S VAN BOTTOM: EACH WAGON HAS ITS OWN STYLE

HAL'S *HAMMAM*

Hal Wynne-Jones: I first came across *hammam* (steam baths) in a small town in Anatolia. The baths opened at five in the morning, and there was no better way to start the day than lying on a scalding marble slab gazing up through the steam at the dawn breaking through the tiny, star-shaped windows.

Next I encountered *savusauna* (smoke sauna) in Finland. The original sauna is a log cabin with a massive stone oven and no chimney. The fire in the oven is lit the day before and the smoke finds its way out through the chinks. The fire is allowed to die and the air to clear before the sauna starts. Everything and everyone is blackened with soot, which is cleaned off with a dip in a frozen lake. As the oven cools, it is used to dry herbs and mushrooms and to air the laundry. They say that if you are ill and you cannot be cured by the sauna, wood tar or *pontika* (illegally brewed spirits, or moonshine), then prepare for the grave.

High in Colorado, I stumbled upon some small round stone hut bases. Thinking they were of native American origin, I asked a local historian about them. He explained that they were sweat lodges built by the Irish railway navvies in the last century.

It struck me that the bath house is essentially what differentiates the state of subsistence from that of luxury. So I made up a yurt complex with sauna, *hammam*, and showers and toured festivals with it for a few years. It was very gratifying, providing something that really made people feel good — even the morning after.

DAVID PEARSON

A MODEST EXTERIOR HIDES THE PANELLED INTERIOR OF HAL'S TRAVELLING SAUNA

My sauna trailer is the latest step in this intrigue with steam. I constructed the framework from an old trailer, some sections of yurt crowns, and slabwood from the local sawmill. I then covered this with waterproof canvas tarpaulin. The water boiler was made from gas bottles by a travelling welder/sculptor friend, and the shower is operated by an old well pump. You put the inlet pipe in a bucket of water, pump furiously, and scream as the jet of cold water from the shower head hits you.

The sauna trailer provides a vital refuge from the grime and stress of travelling. With only an armful of firewood and a bucket of rainwater, it can be up and running in half an hour.

THE WELLS FAMILY FIDDLERS

Linda Wells: We love our home on wheels lifestyle. Our family, myself, Orbie, Caleb, 14, Isaac, 11, and Elijah Kole, 6, enjoy going from place to place and meeting new friends. Since Orbie had to work away from home so much for his job of trimming trees out of the power lines, we decided to get a bus so the whole family could be together.

We bought our first bus in 1986 to be converted. We took the seats out and made our own customized rolling home. This allowed us to travel as we pleased and we were able to camp out at the various lakes, rivers, and coasts along our way.

In 1989, while traveling through Pendleton, Oregon, our son Isaac was born in the bus. So, instead of only home birth, we also believe in bus birthing. Orbie has since retired and now helps with the home schooling of our children.

In 1996 we bought our third bus, a 1980 International School Bus, 35 feet (11 m) long, and made another rolling home. In this bus we put in two sets of bunk beds, a queen size bed, sinks, counters, tables, and cupboards. This was our own design, including a water system, a battery system with inverter, and an electrical system. The whole family helped to paint the bus in different shades of green.

We love to go to the mountains just to see God's creations. The bus allows us to pull off on just about any back road to camp. We usually meet new people and have made many new friends. Last year we went to Quartzsite, Arizona to spend the winter. There was no snow, unlike at our

GREG THOMAS

THE WELLS FAMILY FIDDLERS BY THEIR ROLLING HOME
LEFT TO RIGHT: ISAAC, KELLY, ORBIE, ELIJAH KOLE, KASEY, AND LINDA

cabin in the hills of Washington, on Cougar Creek, near Republic. While in Arizona, the entire family took up fiddle playing. I learned to play, and now teach the boys and granddaughters Kelly and Kasey, who travel along with the family in the summer time. We find time while we sit around the campfire to practise songs like Baby Doll, The Tennessee Waltz, Amazing Grace, and many other gospel favorites.

Our family travels to many different places and one of our favorites is the Oregon Coast. In August we are hosted by Greg Thomas (www.school-busconversions.com) in a campsite surrounded by fir trees, overlooking the Salmon River. Here we pitch in with chores to maintain the site, so it stays beautiful all year. While traveling, we usually find local jobs such as waiting

tables, working at McDonald's, picking berries, cutting firewood, and making all sorts of arts and crafts to sell. Often we find ourselves at barter fairs, where the family sells beaded jewelry, soap and homemade remedies, which I craft from recipes that have passed through the family for many generations.

The best reason for having a home on wheels is the opportunity to meet many people from all walks of life. We always have a place to park and call home, no matter where we are, or who we are with. We love being mobile and just going wherever we want to, which at this time means going to various Old Time Fiddling events. As they say: The Good Lord willing, and the creek don't rise (at least one that the bus can't go through), we'll continue our rolling home lifestyle.

GREG THOMAS

JAY BECK

TOP: THE WELLS FAMILY'S THIRD CONVERSION – A 1980 INTERNATIONAL SCHOOLBUS
BOTTOM: SCHOOLBUS BEFORE CONVERSION

PURE AND SIMPLE

Jay Shafer: In 1994 I bought a 17 foot (5 m) Airstream, gutted it, refurbished it, and moved in. I was simplifying my life by reducing the amount of space I inhabited and getting rid of everything that would not fit into my new home.

But simplification is a complicated process. My definition of necessity includes everything indispensable to my *contented* survival, so a television, video, and CD player were integral to my home's design. I also installed some extra insulation, a composting toilet, and a solar panel.

I chose an Airstream because of its streamlined aesthetic. The shells of these trailers look like yesterday's idea of the future without looking dated, but the inside of mine was pure 1964. The orange shag carpeting, lime green Formica countertop, and floral pattern polyester upholstery had to go. Some might have seen the original interior as desirable in a retro sort of way, but in my new, more natural life there was no room for so many synthetics. I replaced the shag with tatami and covered most everything else with pine tongue-and-groove. The place looked like the inside of a wooden barrel, and I loved it.

As it turned out, the insulation I had installed wasn't quite enough for my comfort in our cold Iowa winters, and the narrow bed insisted on too much intimacy with overnight guests or none at all. So, after three years of mostly contented living in my little Airstream, I began building another place on wheels, of about the same size.

My advice to anyone setting out to simplify – remember that even minimalism can get excessive.

JAY SHAAFER

THE AIRSTREAM'S TIMELESS DESIGN AND STREAMLINED AESTHETIC ARE UNSURPASSED
IN THE RECREATIONAL VEHICLE INDUSTRY

THE HOMESTEAD

Paul James: My 1935 Winchester 15 foot (4.5 m) 4-berth caravan, with a lantern roof, was delivered to me on a very wet and foggy day in November 1994, full of woodworm, rot, and holes.

Restoration started on New Year's Day 1995, when I removed the wheels and lowered the caravan on to bulks of timber, to keep the structure "square". On close inspection most of the panelling needed replacing. The first step was to spray the whole van with woodworm treatment.

I started working on the roof and then tackled the walls. One at a time I removed the panels, using each one as a pattern to cut a new one, and repairing the frame as necessary, until the van was completely repanelled. Next I waterproofed the roof and fitted new windows and doors.

The oak-faced ply interior panels had suffered from woodworm and water leaks, so these were replaced, one by one. When I got down to the wooden chassis I found lots of rot, so I had to splice new wood to the front end and renew the front cross member. Finally I stained the interior wood light oak and replaced the mattresses, covers, curtains, and carpet. We named the caravan "The Homestead", as it is an extension of our home.

For the past ten years we have towed The Homestead all over Britain with a 1933 Morris Oxford saloon. We exhibit at shows and fairs and use it for holidays, towing with a modern car on the longer trips. Wherever we are, someone will tell us of their seaside holidays as a child in a similar caravan — it evokes many fond memories.

PAUL JAMES

TOP: THE RENOVATED 1933 MORRIS OXFORD PULLS THE REFURBISHED 1934 WINCHESTER SPECIAL
BOTTOM: THE CARAVAN BEFORE RENOVATION

THE OREGON WAGON TRAIN

Laura Huggins: Creak of leather, grinding and crunching of steel-rimmed wooden wheels, and the steady plodding of horses' hooves on hard-baked earth fill the air. Ahead, the wagon ruts left from tens of thousands of covered immigrant wagons and handcarts pointed for Oregon, California, and the Salt Lake Valley seem to go on forever through the sea of rock and sagebrush.

You can almost hear the voices of the men, women, and children who dreamed and suffered and died along this wild and lonely trail. It is somehow hard to fathom that this unassuming track is the highway of America's Great Western Expansion – the place where the idea Manifest Destiny and reality became one. When you crossed the high and windy plains and through South Pass, a gap in the Wind River Mountains known as the "doorway to destiny", it was a journey where you moved into the future you had always dreamed of.

Traveling this trail stirs up a mixture of emotion: wonder at the vastness of it all, amazement at the hardships immigrants must have suffered. And one can only imagine the despair that tens of miles of water-less "Great American Desert" might have fostered. The mind is sobered by knowing that all along this trail lie the unmarked graves of those whose dreams led them to this windswept place, where cholera, accident, or some other misfortune ended their quest.

As this trail traverses Wyoming it is little changed since the time of its heyday, when long immigrant trains of prairie schooners and undaunted pony

RYAN SCHMIDT

ON THE OREGON TRAIL, THE RUTS LEFT BY TENS OF THOUSANDS OF WAGONS
SEEM TO GO ON FOREVER

express riders traveled on it. It still lies remote from most of human habitation, a place of solace to the antelope and prairie dogs. It is a vast and open wilderness which beckons to the urge to explore within us.

The wagon train follows a small section of the Oregon Trail for a week. We would camp along the Sweetwater River or along the many small streams that feed it. We would visit lonely graves and memorials to those who perished, experience the impermanence of the gold boom fever, see the fantastic shapes of the Oregon Buttes, and on the last day, cross South Pass itself into "Oregon Territory" – now divided into Oregon, Washington, Idaho, and Wyoming. Days for visitors to the trail are spent much like the days of travelers of old, riding horseback or in the wagon. We enjoy far more safety and the certain knowledge that plenty of ice water, tea, or lemonade and a meal lie at the end of our day's travel. Some who wish to have the authentic experience spend part of their day walking along the dusty track in the wake of the lumbering wagons.

Evenings along the trail are spent enjoying some things that immigrants also enjoyed, like listening to a tall tale told by an old-timer, and others that were outside trail amenities, like the little modern luxuries that await the weary traveler at the end of the day. Guests can take some time to clean up in the creek or river, snooze in their tents before a hearty "traditional trail" dinner, or visit with other "immigrants". We are encouraged to keep a journal as so many original immigrants did. Our hosts make this easy by giving us a canvas-covered booklet filled with excerpts from original trail journals as well as blank pages, so that we might each make our own voice part of the "voices from the trail".

One of the nights is spent camped at the Willie's Handcart Memorial, where many Mormon immigrants perished in an unseasonably early snowstorm. It is a place that drives home the fact that so many lost their lives in pursuit of a dream. We also visit the 1860s gold boom town of South Pass City, home of women's suffrage. Women in the west were far outnumbered by men, sometimes by 20 to 1. They hunted for food and cleared the land for building homes, and were still expected to have the traditional roles

RYAN SCHMIDT

of mother, homemaker, and nurse. They fought for a decent environment to bring up their families, and "civilized" the West. These women were given the right to vote far earlier than many of their sisters around the country.

At night, the campfire fights the dark as we gather around its warmth and light. Conversation and music are some of the "tastes of the trail" that we enjoy. The silhouettes of the cowboys and the plaintive songs of the guitars take us back to that dream of the "Red River Valley" and our days "Home on the Range". The scent of burning sagebrush fills the air, as it must have 150 years ago, emitted by numerous night fires that filled the wagon ring. One by one, weary travelers make their way to their tipi lodging and sleeping bag. Sounds of coyotes and night birds fill the air and the sky is ablaze with the light of a million stars. We drift into sleep, knowing that tomorrow brings another day of travel along the immigrant way.

TOP: GENTLE HORSES PULL THE COVERED WAGONS UNDER THE BIG SKY
BELOW: THE TRAVELER CAN TAKE A TURN TO DRIVE

RESTFULNESS AND MOTION

Dan Wing: Why is our wagon such an object of admiration and emotional release for those who see or stay in it? I think it is the combination of opposites that it represents. The essence of our wagon is its combination of sweetness and wild improbability, fantasy and utility, restfulness and motion. How can it be such a satisfying, archetypal form to so many people who have never seen an actual Gypsy wagon?

We hadn't seen one, either, but with guidance from Jim Tolpin who has built several wagons (see page 58), and with a set of plans for a 1914 wagon (which we followed only in spirit) we came up with a combination that "works". We used the ledge shape and sloping sides of many English wagons, the panelled front and smooth sides of a French wagon we saw in a magazine, and lots of recycled but distinctive pieces — antique wheels, cupboards, door, and window trim — that gave an older character than we would have achieved with all new materials.

I put the wagon on four wheels, distributed as they would have been on an original wagon. Another choice was to use the platform of the floor and its rim-joists, glued and screwed, to provide the structure of the wagon, with only a modest strip of metal running around and across it, to which the spring perches are welded. They get most of their security from being bolted up to the rim-joists and lower sheathing. Building the wagon in this way, using plywood judiciously and invisibly, kept it light enough to pull with an antique truck, which is hard to achieve with a full trailer frame and the

DAN WING

TRAVELING LIGHT – DAN'S ANTIQUE TRUCK PULLS HIS STYLISH LIGHTWEIGHT WAGON
THROUGH TIMELESSLY WILD AND BEAUTIFUL LANDSCAPE

wagon box just bolted on. Also, we put translucent insulated panels into the roof to get great light into the wagon. We insulated the rest of the roof with flexible foam under the cover, keeping us warm in the spring and fall but (more importantly) cool in the summer. We decided: one bed, no toilet. We did not want our sweet wagon to be cobbled up with a bunch of pipes, levers, doors, and tricks.

What are the best things? Well, tea parties for little girls are great, with our miniature cups and pots, the girls in kerchiefs, beads, and long dresses. The Caravan Reading Club is a favorite summer activity for slightly older neighborhood kids, so they don't forget their lessons. It has been loaned for more "grown-up" summer parties in a hillside orchard, where champagne was poured from the window and the light from lanterns played on the trees. One couple even spent their wedding night in the wagon, parked between a hayfield and a garden.

When out on the road and far from home, we meet people we would never otherwise meet, and we go where we would not otherwise go — as when we were asked by Amish farmers to stay a few days and help harvest the oats at the end of a golden summer; or when we camped in a ring of tipis on an old Spanish grant on a mesa in New Mexico; or when we angled our wagon into a grove of pines above a California cliff so that night after night through the open door, we could see the sun go down into the Pacific, aware all night of the crash of rollers on the beach below. Heaven.

DAN WING

TOP: A GOOD PLACE FOR DREAMING   BOTTOM LEFT: COPPER AND BRASS KITCHEN FITTINGS
BOTTOM RIGHT: REAR VIEW OF THE GYPSY WAGON

TYPES OF WAGON

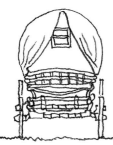

Pot cart

Open-Lot

Choosing to acquire or build a special handmade wagon or historic caravan is different from owning a conventional or modern recreational vehicle (RV) or trailer. Older models need to be treated with care and respect and are unlikely to do all the things a brand new model can do. But this does depend on the type and how well it has been maintained or renovated. Well-restored vintage Airstreams have proved very durable and can go almost anywhere. But it is unlikely that many today will use a horse-drawn Romany-style *vardo* except for an organized vacation on quiet country roads or to visit annual Gypsy fairs. It all depends what you want a living wagon for – hobby project, picturesque extra bedroom, office, playroom, or guestroom in your garden or backyard, or caravan to live in and take on the road.

A static showpiece is the simplest option as the wagon does not need to be roadworthy. But if you want to use it on the road, then safety is paramount. You should seek professional advice on the undercarriage and how the total laden weight relates to how it is to be towed – by horse or car/truck. The age of the towing vehicle may also be a consideration, as owners often like to tow their hand-built wagon or historic caravan with an antique or vintage vehicle.

All these factors affect the wagon type, its total weight, size, and materials. For horse-drawn options, lightness and compactness are

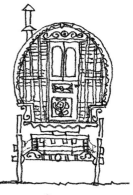

Bowtop

Reading

Ledge

vital. Once you have decided on the type and size, you need to think about whether to renovate an older model or build/commission a new one. Ecologically, it is preferable to renovate rather than build new, as less materials and energy will be used. You will also be saving a small and valuable part of a vanishing heritage. But for new work, ensure that you use sustainable and non-toxic materials and as many recycled materials as possible. For restoration work, seek help from specialist clubs and use traditional methods (see Resources).

Whatever option you choose, you need to be aware of the main types of traditional living wagons. These are the Reading, Burton, Ledge, Bowtop, and Open-Lot. The Bowtop has a rounded top with canvas stretched over wooden "bows" and is ideal for renovation. The Open-Lot, a newer variant, has an open front with posts and canvas curtains instead of a wall and door, and is the lightest and simplest version to build (pages 82–3). Even smaller is the two- or four-wheeled tilted Pot cart (traditionally used by potters to carry their wares), which although not strictly a living wagon, is sometimes used as such by modern travellers. The Reading, built by Dunton & Sons of Reading, England – the pride of many a Romany family – has straight wooden-ribbed sides that slope slightly outward from bottom to top. Its large rear wheels are set outside the body. The Ledge is similar, but to give more space inside its sides are built out on "ledges" over the wheels (pages 84–5). The Burton – a show folk rather than Gypsy wagon – gains even more floor space by building the whole floor out over smaller wheels. If you can find one, they make wonderful restoration projects (see pages 28–33).

Burton

MAKING AN OPEN-LOT

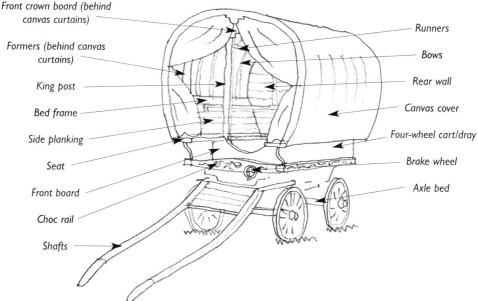

Front crown board (behind canvas curtains)

Formers (behind canvas curtains)

King post

Bed frame

Side planking

Seat

Front board

Choc rail

Shafts

Runners

Bows

Rear wall

Canvas cover

Four-wheel cart/dray

Brake wheel

Axle bed

I Fit boards and seats

2 Build end deck

To build an Open-Lot Bowtop you first need a sturdy wooden four-wheel spring cart (sometimes called a dray, trolley, or bogey) and a pair of shafts. To allow enough space to live and sleep in, yet be light enough to be horse-drawn, the cart should not be larger than 9 feet (2.75 m) long and 5 feet (1.5 m) wide. Check that the front wheels have a "fore-carriage" that can turn full lock.

Before you start to build the top, do as wagon-builder Walter Lloyd (see page 34) does and "draw the shape of the front or back of the wagon full scale on a wall, to get the shape just right". Start by

3 Add front frame

4 Fix roof runners

screwing and bolting front, back, and side boards to the cart floor, remembering to leave a small space for a porch at the front. Fix two seat boards at each side and strengthen with brackets. Next, build the rear wall on the ground with half-inch (1 cm) tongue-and-groove boarding screwed firmly to two upright king posts. Cut out a small window opening and then bolt the whole deck to the cart. Finally, fix the crown board, cut to the prescribed bowtop curve. For the front, bolt the two upright king posts to the front board and to the crown board. (As this is an open-lot, no cross boarding is fitted at the front.)

For the roof, fix "runners" to the back and front crown boards. Add curved "formers" to complete the front, fixing lightweight tongue-and-groove boarding part-way up each side. The most difficult part is the fitting of the "bows". Use slim lengths of straight-grained, knot-free softwood, soaked in water for about a week so they will bend. Screw one end to the top runner and then, as Walter Lloyd does, gently pull the bow downward using boiling water to help it bend, screwing it to each runner in turn and finally to the seat edge. Don't worry if some break and have to be done again – it happens to the best wagon-builder!

Finally, build the bed frame at the back, fit a window with shutters, and cover the top with an insulated inner lining and a tight-fitting green cotton canvas sheet. Add cupboards and a small stove inside, and let your imagination run riot in carving and decorating the outside, to complete your own Bowtop.

For detailed information see *How to Build a Bow Top* by Walter Lloyd, listed in Further Reading on page 95.

5 Add sides and bows

6 Fit bed and cover

MAKING A LEDGE

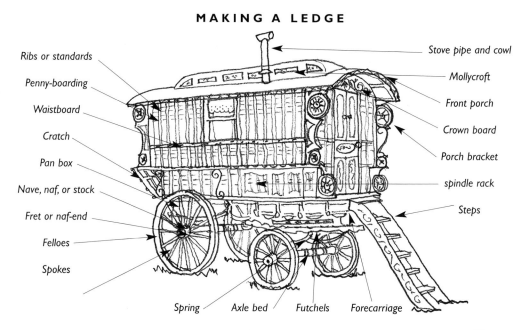

Ribs or standards

Penny-boarding

Waistboard

Cratch

Pan box

Nave, naf, or stock

Fret or naf-end

Felloes

Spokes

Spring   Axle bed   Futchels   Forecarriage

Stove pipe and cowl

Mollycroft

Front porch

Crown board

Porch bracket

spindle rack

Steps

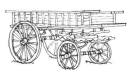

1 Build underworks

Building a Ledge is complicated. They can be commissioned from professional wagon-builders such as Andy Ball (page 48) or Jim Tolpin (page 58). It is more likely that you will want to try your hand at renovation. It is a good idea to have an old caravan checked over by a professional before purchase. Two aspects are vital: the underworks ("unders") and the timber. If either is deficient, the entire wagon is at risk. The "unders" – wheels, axles, springs, frame, and steering fore-carriage – define the wagon's safety and smooth running. Find an experienced wagon builder to do any repairs to the wheels and undercarriage if you plan to use the caravan on the road.

2 Fix front and end walls

And remember that the traditional Ledge was designed to be horse drawn, so if you want a car-towed version, you will need to consult a specialist wagon-builder.

To build a Ledge all wood must be knot-free and thoroughly seasoned, with time allowed for second shrinkage after pieces have been sawn to shape. An expert wagon-builder will start with the wheels – elm hub ("stocks"), oak spokes, ash rims ("felloes"), and iron tyres. Next come the lathe-turned axle-cases (traditionally made by specialist firms). These are attached to the fore-carriage at the front and hind-carriage at the back via springs and "scrole-irons". The fore-carriage or "lock" (a curved structure of ash members ("futchels") to which the shafts are attached) enables steering via two well-greased steel ring plates – one fixed to the fore-carriage and one to the underside of the wagon floor.

Once the two undercarriages are bolted to the oak floor frame, the upper part of the caravan can be built. Using pine for lightness, the lower walls and ledges come first. Then, above these, the main walls are built of upright ribs ("standards") chamfered for lightness, with tongue-and-groove boarding on the inside – the lightest being "penny-boarding", the width of an old English penny. Once the front and rear walls are topped with carved crown boards, the curved roof and characteristic "Mollycroft" skylight can be added. Finally, to finish the exterior, distinctive porch brackets are carved and fitted, and then the double door, sash windows, louvred shutters, and entry steps. The interior cupboards, stove, and bed, plus extra elaborate carving and painting inside and out, complete your Ledge.

3 Add side walls

4 Build roof frame

5 Finish roof and "Mollycroft"

INTERIORS

If you are building your own wagon you can choose and design a modern interior (see page 88) or you can adapt a traditional Romany layout (see page 89). Although every Romany family had its individual preferences, a fairly standard tried-and-tested *vardo* layout evolved over the years. A rear bed space, lit by a small casement or bay window, has a cupboard/closet beneath for storing bedding and also doubles as a second berth. Bench seats along both sides, with lockers beneath,

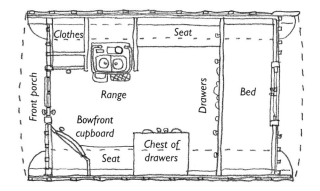

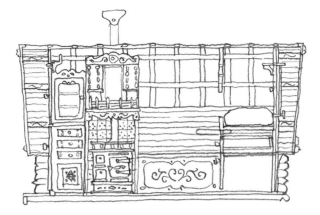

provide sitting space, while sliding surfaces under the top berth provide table space. All cupboards/closets are built in and are finely carved and decorated. These comprise a chest of drawers, a tall bowfront cupboard with curved glass door, and a wardrobe unit.

A cast-iron range with oven and hobs, such as the popular "Hostess", is situated on the offside (so the chimney clears tree branches). It has a finely carved and tiled surround with brass-railed mantelpiece and engraved mirror above. Although the range was sometimes used for cooking, most was done outside in a bender tent.

Considering the minimal space, living in a small well-equipped wagon can be surprisingly comfortable and satisfying.

UNIQUE SOLUTIONS

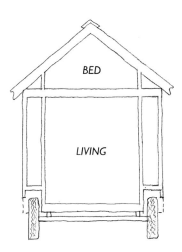

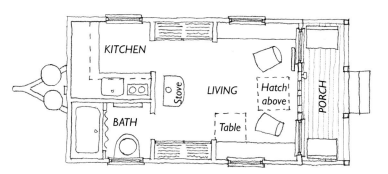

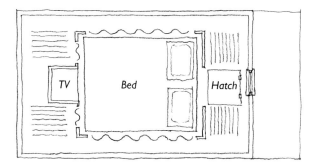

Tumbleweed, designed and built by Jay
Shafer (page 16) is 17 feet (5.25 m) long,
8 feet 6 inches (2.6 m) wide, and 13 feet
6 inches (4 m) high. This novel house design
has every facility – living space (with out-
door porch), bathroom with shower, kitchen,
bed loft, and plenty of storage. It also has a
composting toilet, photovoltaic electricity,
and a propane gas stove. For extra strength
the stud-frame walls are screwed-and-glued
to ply sheathing and metal hurricane clips
secure the roof rafters firmly to the walls.

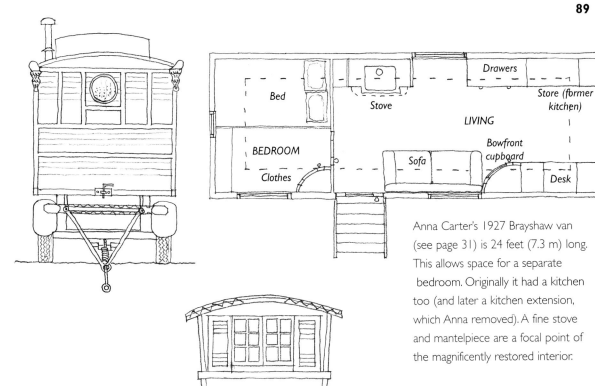

Anna Carter's 1927 Brayshaw van
(see page 31) is 24 feet (7.3 m) long.
This allows space for a separate
bedroom. Originally it had a kitchen
too (and later a kitchen extension,
which Anna removed). A fine stove
and mantelpiece are a focal point of
the magnificently restored interior.

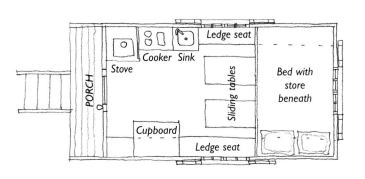

Dan Wing's elegant hand-crafted Ledge wagon
(see page 76) is 16 feet (4.9 m) long, 8 feet
(2.4 m) wide, and just over 10 feet (3 m) high.
It has a similar interior layout to a traditional
vardo but incorporates a modern cooker and
copper sink. The wagon is designed to be easily
towed by a car or small truck.

DECORATIONS

A traditional Romany *vardo* would not be considered complete unless it was decorated – carved, painted, and even gilded. Today, elaborate decoration is out of fashion. Unadorned fine lines and structural beauty are more appreciated. But it depends on what your wagon or caravan is for. If you own an historic example, you will probably want to restore the decorations lovingly to their original beauty. If you are building a reproduction wagon as a hobby, you may want to finish it in style also. You might want to create a showpiece to attract attention, and surely it will! The more you decorate, the more your wagon will stand out and be a focus of attention. So, if you wish to avoid being pestered by photographers, opt for a more subdued and subtle approach.

Traditional wagon carving was not applied arbitrarily – it appeared to grow out of the structure. It also lightened the weight. Reaching

Wright wagon door

Hill wagon door

Porch brackets

Dunton

Varney

Wright

Crown Boards

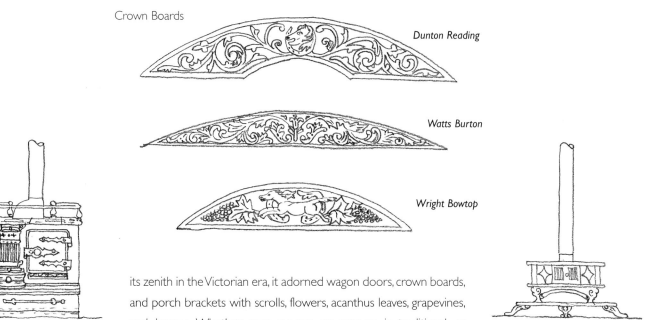

Dunton Reading

Watts Burton

Wright Bowtop

Hostess stove

its zenith in the Victorian era, it adorned wagon doors, crown boards, and porch brackets with scrolls, flowers, acanthus leaves, grapevines, and horses. Whether your wagon or caravan is traditional or modern, use your imagination, but remember that the decorations need to match its basic design and style.

Queenie stove

Brayshaw decoration

Scrolls (after Walter Lloyd)

RESOURCES

NOTE ON TELEPHONE NUMBERS
For national calls, *do not* dial the country code inside the first pair of brackets. Dial the prefix inside the second pair, followed by the rest of the number.

For international calls to Europe, dial the country code inside the first pair of brackets, but *not* the European prefix (0) inside the second pair. Follow this up with the rest of the number.

For international calls to the US, dial the whole number including all prefixes. Note that numbers beginning with 800 are free inside the US only.

SHOWFOLK'S LIVING VANS
National Fairground Archive
Main Library
University of Sheffield
Sheffield
S10 2TN
UK
Tel: (00 44) (0)114 222 7231
Fax: (00 44) (0)114 273 9826
Collection of photographs, printed, manuscript, and audio-visual material, covering all aspects of the culture of travelling showpeople.

ROMANY MUSEUM
Gordon Boswell
Clay Lake
Spalding
Lincolnshire
PE12 6BL
UK
Tel: (00 44) (0)1775 710599
www.leapreston.demon.co.uk

GYPSY CARAVANS
For Gypsy caravan holidays look for "Romany Gypsy Caravans" on the world wide web.

Gypsy Lore Society
5607 Greenleaf Road
Cheverly
MD20785
USA
www.gypsyloresociety.org/
Founded in the UK in 1888, based in the USA since 1989. Promotes the study of Gypsy, Traveler, and analagous peripatetic cultures worldwide.

Gypsy Collections at the University of Liverpool, UK
http://sca.lib.liv.ac.uk/
collections/gypsy/intro.htm
Includes the Gypsy Lore Society Archives and the Scott Macfie Gypsy Collection of books, manuscripts, prints, photos, sound recordings, and press cuttings.

The Patrin Web Journal: Romani Culture and History
www.geocities.com/Paris/5121/patrin.htm

Articles and links to relevant organizations.

MICROCARAVANS
Steve Pepper
Microcaravan News and International Register of Microcaravans (IROM)
42 Charles Avenue
Harrogate
HG1 4PE
UK
www.trikes.freeserve.co.uk/irom/list.htm

THE ROYAL BERKSHIRE STEAM FAIR
Carter's Yard
White Waltham
nr Maidenhead
Berkshire
SL6 3LW
UK
Tel: (00 44) (0)1628 822221
Available for private and film hire, promotional work, and corporate entertainment.

SAUNA TRAILER
Hal Wynne-Jones
Hullasey Barn
Tarlton
Cirencester
Gloucestershire
England, UK
Tel/Fax:
(00 44) (0)1285 770773
Yurts for sale. May be hired out for functions, parties, etc.

SCHOOLBUS CONVERSIONS
Greg Thomas
PO Box 144
Rose Lodge
Oregon 97372
USA
Tel: (00 1) 541 994 4277
www.
SchoolBusConversions.com
For the DIY motorhome fan.

HIDDEN TRAILS
Hidden Trails
202-380 West 1st Ave
Vancouver
BC V5Y 3T7
Canada
Tel: (00 1) 604 323 1141
Fax: (00 1) 604 323 1148
http://hiddentrails.com
Over 300 riding destinations.

PROFESSIONAL WAGON BUILDERS

Walter Lloyd
Fair View Lane
Staveley-in-Cartmel
Ulverston
Cumbria
LA12 8NS
UK
Tel: (00 44) (0)1539 531181

John Shervell
Traditional Shepherds' Huts
Bendish Farm
Bendish
Hitchin
Hertfordshire
SG4 8JJ
UK
www.
traditionalshepherdshuts.co.uk

Andy Ball
Weaver's Workshops
The Street
Uley
Gloucestershire
GL11 5AG
Tel/fax:
(00 44) (0)1453 860866
http://members.aol.com/and
chain/gloswheelandcarriage
.html

Jim Tolpin
820 Polk Street
Port Townsend
WA98368
USA
email: jimtolpin@hotmail.com
www.cottagehome.net

Dan Wing
The Cookeville Garage
PO Box 473
Corinth
VT 05039
USA
Willing to build wagons similar
to the one on page 77.

VINTAGE CARAVANS

The Historic Caravan Club
"Arwel"
Victoria Road
Llanwrtd Wells
Powys
LD5 4SU
UK
http://homepage.ntlworld.com/
msmith/index.htm
Promotes restoration,
preservation, use, and display
of early historic caravans.

Period & Classic Caravan Club
128 Fulbourn Old Drift
Cherry Hinton
Cambridge
CB1 9LR
UK
Tel: (00 44) (0)1223 248187

Teardrop caravans
www.teardrops.net

Retro Camping Club de
France
http://rccf.w3to

Vintage Airstream Club
Membership Chair
PO Box 4173
Windam
NH 03087
USA
www.airstream.net/index.html
For restorers, travelers, and
enthusiasts.

Wally Byam Caravan Club
International
PO Box 612
Jackson Center
OH 45334
USA
Tel: (00 1) 937 596 5211
Fax: (00 1) 937 596 5542
www.wbcci.org/
Provides travel opportunities
for Airstream owners, with
rallies all over the world.

www.vintage-vacations.com
Click on "links"

GENERAL

Association for Environment
Conscious Building
www.aecb.net/index.htm

Ecological Design Association
www.edaweb.org
email:
ecological@designassociation
.freeserve.co.uk
Founded by David Pearson.
Publishes *EcoDesign* magazine.

Friends, Families and Travellers
Advice and Information Unit
Community Base
113 Queens Road
Brighton
BN1 3XG
UK
Tel: (00 44) (0)1273 234 777

Gaiam Real Goods
Solar Living Center
PO Box 836
Hopland
California 95449
USA
Tel: (00 1) 800 919 2400
www.realgoods.com
email: Techs@realgoods.com

www.buildinggreen.com
Site for *Environmental Building
News.*

www.ecotecture.com
Online journal of ecological
design.

INDEX

Bold page numbers refer to photographs and illustrations

FURTHER READING

Braithwaite, Paul *A Palace on Wheels* Carters
Books, Carter's Yard, White Waltham, nr
Maidenhead, Berkshire SL6 3LW, UK, 1999
Tel: (00 44) (0)1628 822221

Groene, J and Groene, G *Living Aboard your RV*
McGraw-Hill, 2002

Jenkinson, Andrew *Caravans: The Story of the British
Trailer Caravans and Their Manufacturers*, Veloce
Publishing plc, 1998

Lane, M and Crotty, J *Mad Monks on the Road*
Simon & Schuster, NY, 1993

Lidz, Jane *Rolling Homes: Handmade Houses on
Wheels* A&W Visual Library, NY 1979

Lloyd, Walter *How to Build a Bowtop*
Woodmanship Ltd, PO Box 12, Carnforth,
Lancashire, LA5 9NN, UK

Old Glory: Vintage Restoration Today ed Peter Kelly,
Issue no. 138, August 2001

Pallidini, Jodi and Dubin, Beverly *Roll your Own*
Collier Books, NY 1974

Shafer, Jay "Tumbleweed" *Designer/Builder* Vol VIII,
No 2, June 2001

The World's Fair
(Magazine about showpeople, fairgrounds, and
living vans)
PO Box 57, Albert Mill, Albert Street, Oldham
OL8 3WF, UK

Ward-Jackson, C.H. and Harvey, Denis E. *The
English Gypsy Caravan* David & Charles, 1972

Wing, Daniel "Gypsy Wagon" *Fine Homebuilding*
Dec 1988/Jan 1989

ACKNOWLEDGMENTS

Gaia Books is deeply indebted to each and
every contributor and photographer of the
stories featured in this book. Gaia Books would
also like to thank the many people who have
helped with freewheeling homes research,
mainly behind the scenes and for no personal
gain: *Vanessa Toulmin from the National Fairground
Archive, Paul Braithwaite, Ingrid Crawford.*

David Pearson would like to thank the Gaia
team: *Pey Colborne* for her tireless work in
researching and compiling the fascinating stories
of the contributors; *Bridget Morley* for her
talented and imaginative design; *Katherine Pate*
for her professional editorial work; *Kate Rogers*
for production control; *Sheila Smith* for
production; *Patrick Nugent* for project manage-
ment, *Deborah Pate* for proofreading, and *Jane
Parker* for the index.

I would also like to thank everyone at
Chelsea Green Publishing for their helpful and
enthusiastic support.

I also wish to acknowledge and commend the
invaluable source: *The English Gypsy Caravan* by
C. H. Ward-Jackson, with the excellent drawings
by Denis Harvey on which the illustrations on
pages 80–81, 86–87, and 90–91 were based.